# FEEDBACK IS NOT A GIFT

## It is a Minefield

### JD Ussery

**Amazon**

"If you can't figure out your purpose, figure out your passion. For your passion will lead you right into your purpose."

T.D. JAKES

# PREFACE

Passion is a powerful and compelling emotion or feeling towards something or someone.

It's often characterized by a strong desire, enthusiasm, or dedication.

It could be a hobby, an activity, a cause, or a profession that significantly stimulates interest and brings immense satisfaction.

Passion often drives individuals to go beyond the ordinary, investing significant amounts of time, effort, and emotion into the pursuits they deeply care about. That intense, driving feeling motivates people to achieve their goals and make a difference.

# Introduction

*Cambridge Dictionary*

<u>Gift:</u> *A present or something that is given without asking for it, on a special occasion, especially to show friendship or say thank you.*

<u>Minefield:</u> *A situation or subject that is very complicated and full of hidden problems and dangers*

Reflect on the recent feedback you've been given. Did it truly feel like a 'gift,' as many claim it to be? Chances are, it felt more like navigating a minefield than receiving a present.

In today's fast-paced and ever-evolving business landscape, effective management and leadership are more critical than ever before. The "Feedback is a Gift" mantra has become a widely accepted and often unquestioned principle. It is repeated in boardrooms, seminars, and leadership workshops as the ultimate solution for fostering growth, enhancing performance, and building strong, cohesive teams. Unfortunately, it has taken on the persona that any form of feedback, no matter how it is delivered, is a valuable present to be cherished and appreciated. It has become a prevailing thought in many organizations.

The idea seems simple and compelling on the surface: Feedback, like a gift or a present, is offered without you asking for it, supposedly with good intentions, and benefits you as the recipient. However, I invite you to challenge the conventional wisdom surrounding this seemingly innocent maxim. First, it makes a couple of assumptions that are not always true:

> The first assumption – it is offered with good intentions.
> The second assumption – it benefits the recipient.
> Then there is the inferred conclusion based on the two assumptions that the recipient must receive and consider the

feedback.

Before I go further, properly delivered and received constructive criticism in the right environment can be valuable for personal and professional development. But blindly accepting that all feedback is like a gift you must be thankful for can lead to unintended consequences. In this book, I would like to explore with you the shortcomings of this seemingly harmless mantra and present a more nuanced approach to feedback that truly unlocks the potential for growth and transformation.

Let's be clear: Most conventional training on feedback does include caveats about not having to accept every piece of advice. However, when these teachings are implemented in organizations, the nuances often get overshadowed. What tends to stick are the catchy slogans—like 'Feedback is a Gift'—often at the expense of the more nuanced guidance.

This book aims to convey the same idea but with added clarity and a bit more punch, highlighting the contrast between the ideal teachings and their real-world applications. Feedback can be a powerful ally for both good and evil and must be approached cautiously and thoughtfully.

This brings me to my simple but profound thesis: "Feedback is not a gift, it is a minefield." You might think, "But wait! A minefield? That sounds too severe." And I would reply, "Nay, nay, good citizen. Just as walking into a minefield requires careful preparation and navigation, so too does delivering and receiving feedback." Granted, most of us wouldn't walk into a minefield regardless of planning.

Don't get me wrong, I'm not saying feedback isn't valuable – it certainly can be. But it can also be harmful. In this book, we'll peel back the layers of the "Feedback is a Gift" concept to reveal its inherent limitations and complexities.

While feedback indeed has the potential to be a valuable tool for personal and professional development, accepting the premise that all feedback is a gift can lead to detrimental consequences for individuals and organizations alike. The truth is that not all feedback is created equal, and its impact on individuals can vary significantly depending on its nature, context, and delivery.

# CHAPTER 1: UNVEILING THE LAYERS

Feedback is a complex tapestry woven from multiple threads, each contributing to its overall design and effect. Rather than a one-dimensional entity, feedback is a multifaceted gem, reflecting light and understanding in countless directions. Its depth and intricacies can greatly affect our perceptions, reactions, and subsequent actions. Often, we may regard feedback as a singular entity, straightforward and unambiguous. Yet, its true power and potential lie in its layers, which shape its reception and influence its outcomes. Join me on a journey to unravel this intricate web as we delve deeper into the nuances that define the world of feedback.

**Layer 1 - Constructive vs. Destructive Feedback:** This is the most fundamental layer. Constructive feedback focuses on providing specific, actionable, and growth-oriented insights. It aims to empower the recipient to improve and excel in their performance. On the other hand, destructive feedback lacks helpful guidance and can hurt, demoralize, and damage an individual's confidence and self-esteem.

**Layer 2 - Delivery and Tone:** Thoughtful, constructive, and private feedback given in a calm, positive, and respectful manner enhances the likelihood of the feedback being accepted and acted upon. Conversely, a rushed, harsh, negative tone can trigger defensiveness and resistance, hindering growth potential.

**Layer 3 - Specificity and Clarity:** Effective feedback is clear, specific, and backed by concrete examples. Vague or ambiguous feedback can leave the recipient unsure of what needs improvement, making it challenging to take meaningful action.

**Layer 4 - Intent and Motive:** The underlying intent and motive behind giving feedback plays a significant role. Feedback offered with genuine care and the intention to support growth is more likely to be received positively. However, giving feedback with hidden agendas or ill intentions, once they are revealed (and they eventually will), can lead to distrust and reluctance to accept future feedback.

**Layer 5 - Relevance and Timeliness:** Feedback relevant to the individual's current goals and performance will resonate with the recipient. Additionally, timely feedback, provided close to the observed behavior, allows for better recall and understanding of the context.

**Layer 6 - Frequency and Consistency:** Feedback consistently provided over time allows individuals to track their progress and continuously improve. Infrequent feedback may lead to missed opportunities for growth and development.

**Layer 7 - Balancing Praise and Critique:** A balanced approach that combines recognition of strengths and accomplishments with guidance for improvement fosters a healthy feedback culture. Praise boosts motivation, while constructive criticism highlights areas for growth.

**Layer 8 - Psychological Safety:** Psychological safety within the feedback environment is crucial. When individuals feel safe to express their thoughts, take risks, and admit mistakes without fear of punishment or judgment, they are more open to receiving feedback and embracing growth.

**Layer 9 - Reciprocity and Feedback Culture:** The culture of feedback within an organization or team influences how feedback is perceived. A culture that promotes open and honest communication, where feedback flows both top-down and bottom-up, nurtures a climate of continuous improvement.

**Layer 10 - Growth Mindset and Attitude:** Finally, the recipient's growth mindset and attitude towards feedback play a significant role. Individuals with a growth mindset view feedback as an opportunity for learning and improvement, while those with a fixed mindset may perceive feedback as a judgment of their inherent abilities.

Recognizing and understanding these layers of feedback allows individuals and teams to foster a more thoughtful and effective feedback culture, where feedback becomes a powerful tool for growth, development, and success. Now we will explore each layer in detail.

## Layer 1: The Dual Nature of Feedback

Feedback, like a double-edged sword, possesses a dual nature that can either uplift or wound. That is the crucial distinction between constructive feedback, which serves as a powerful catalyst for growth, and destructive criticism, which can inflict emotional distress and undermine an individual's confidence. By unraveling this essential difference, we lay the groundwork for a more discerning and informed approach to feedback that celebrates its value while questioning its intent and impact.

## Understanding Constructive Feedback

Constructive criticism, often considered the cornerstone of effective feedback practices, holds the potential to ignite personal and professional growth. When delivered thoughtfully and focused on improvement, constructive feedback acts as a mirror, reflecting an individual's strengths and areas for development. It offers specific insights, actionable suggestions, and encouragement, empowering individuals to leverage their strengths and embrace opportunities for growth.

Consider the following: In a highly productive sales team, the manager provides constructive feedback to Sarah, a team member. The manager highlights Sarah's excellent interpersonal skills and ability to build rapport with clients, which has led to numerous successful sales. Simultaneously, the manager points out that Sarah could further enhance her closing techniques by refining her negotiation strategies and provides specific examples that may help in her next sale. Knowing that Sarah is a visual learner, the manager provides charts and drawings to help explain the ideas. Encouraged by this valuable feedback, Sarah attends a negotiation training workshop and subsequently has a remarkable improvement in her sales performance.

Constructive feedback aligns with the principles of positive reinforcement. When individuals receive recognition and encouragement for their strengths and accomplishments, they are motivated to continue excelling in those areas and seek opportunities for further growth.

**Unpacking Destructive Criticism**

On the other end of the feedback spectrum lies destructive criticism, a force capable of inflicting harm and demotivating individuals. Destructive criticism lacks the constructive elements and often involves hurtful language, personal attacks, or vague accusations. It fails to provide guidance for improvement and instead diminishes an individual's sense of self-worth and confidence.

Let's review a different scenario: John receives feedback from his supervisor, which contains negative comments about his work performance, such as calling him "incompetent" and "unreliable." The supervisor fails to offer specific examples or guidance for improvement, leaving John feeling demoralized and disheartened. As a result, John's motivation and productivity decline significantly.

Why, in the "Wide, Wide World of Sports," would John need to consider that feedback a gift? Probably because he took a course or read a book that told him all feedback is a gift. So instead of taking that gift to the nearest toilet and hitting the flush handle, John is left dealing with a stinking pile of crap. (That's right, I said it). Destructive criticism is closely tied to threats to an individual's self-esteem, triggering defensive mechanisms and emotional distress. Such feedback can activate the fight-or-flight response, leading individuals to avoid future feedback interactions and stifle their growth.

You might think that a manager would never do that – they would never frame a conversation that way. I would respond *You're not from around here, are ya*? In my experience, I've seen managers, even senior leadership, do this. Why? Well, that answer could probably be a book unto itself. On occasion, a good manager can simply have a bad day, but, in my humble opinion, sometimes people are promoted to leadership because of their functional or business skills, not their people skills. So, you wind up with a person whose primary job is leading and managing people, yet they are ill-equipped to do so. Until those folks are adequately mentored and trained in the art of leadership and constructive criticism, destructive feedback can be the expected result. And sometimes, you just run across people with the personalities to match the northern end of a south-bound mule.

As we study the complexities of feedback, it becomes evident that a balanced approach is essential for creating a feedback culture that fosters growth and empowerment. Emphasizing the importance of constructive criticism while being mindful of the detrimental impact of destructive feedback lays the foundation for a discerning feedback culture.

## A Culture of Balanced Feedback

In a balanced feedback approach, managers and team members are trained to provide feedback that combines praise for achievements with specific areas for improvement. This balanced feedback helps individuals recognize their strengths while encouraging them to strive for excellence in their developmental areas.

A balanced feedback approach aligns with the principles of

a growth mindset. Individuals with a growth mindset view feedback as an opportunity to learn and improve, embracing challenges and valuing effort as a path to mastery.

As we recognize the dual nature of feedback, we pave the way for a more thoughtful and discerning approach. Embracing a balanced feedback culture empowers individuals and organizations to unleash its transformative power, fostering personal and collective growth.

Together, let us challenge the oversimplified notion of feedback as a one-size-fits-all gift and embrace a more nuanced approach that propels individuals and organizations toward unparalleled success.

**References:**

1. Dweck, C. S. (2006). Mindset: The New Psychology of Success. New York: Ballantine Books.

2. Grant, A. M., & Ashford, S. J. (2008). The dynamics of proactivity at work. Research in Organizational Behavior, 28, 3-34.

3. Sosik, J. J., & Dinger, S. L. (2007). Relationships between leadership style and vision content: The moderating role of need for social approval, self-monitoring, and need for social power. The Leadership Quarterly, 18(2), 134-153.

**Layer 2: Delivery and Tone - The Art of Empathy and Respect**

The tone and delivery of feedback can significantly influence how it is received and processed by the recipient. For this layer, we explore how empathy, respect, and emotional intelligence used as an artful and thoughtful delivery vehicle can transform feedback from merely exchanging information into a powerful tool for growth and empowerment.

Delivery and tone are vital components when giving feedback, as they can significantly influence how the feedback is received and acted upon. Let's break down each:

## Delivery

**Clarity**: It's essential to be clear and specific when giving feedback. Vague feedback can lead to confusion and misunderstandings.

**Constructiveness**: Feedback should aim at helping the individual grow and improve. Rather than just pointing out what's wrong, offer solutions or ways to improve.

**Timeliness**: Feedback is best given soon after the event so the incident or situation is fresh in memory.

**Private Setting**: Depending on the nature of the feedback, it might be best delivered privately to avoid embarrassment.

**Non-accusatory Language**: Using "I" statements instead of "you" statements can reduce defensiveness. For example, "I noticed that the report had some inconsistencies," rather than "You made errors in the report."

**Balanced**: Including positive feedback with negative can make it easier to digest. This approach also ensures that individuals understand what they're doing well and areas where they might need improvement.

## Tone

**Calmness**: Your voice should be calm and even, not emotional or heated.

**Positivity**: Even if the feedback is negative, a positive or neutral tone can make it more palatable. This doesn't mean sugarcoating but rather conveying hope and confidence that the individual can improve.

**Respect**: Always show respect for the person receiving the feedback. Avoid using a condescending or sarcastic tone.

**Empathy**: Show that you understand where they're coming from. This might mean acknowledging their efforts or the challenges they face.

**Consistency**: Your tone should match your message. If you're giving positive feedback, your tone should be uplifting. If you're addressing a concern, your tone should be more serious but still respectful.

In summary, how feedback is delivered can be as important as the feedback itself. The right delivery and tone can make the difference between feedback that is accepted and acted upon or that's dismissed and leads to defensiveness. To be effective, feedback should be provided in a manner that helps the recipient recognize its value and motivates them.

### The Human Touch in Feedback

We must recognize that feedback is not solely about the content of the message but also about the human connection forged through delivery and tone. A positive, supportive, and empathetic delivery empowers individuals to embrace feedback as an opportunity for growth and development. Conversely, a harsh tone can inadvertently create barriers to learning and improvement.

By mastering the art of empathy, emotional intelligence, and respectful communication, leaders and feedback providers can enhance the effectiveness of their feedback.

### References:

1. Deci, E. L., & Ryan, R. M. (2000). The "what" and "why" of goal pursuits: Human needs and the self-determination of behavior. Psychological Inquiry, 11(4), 227-268.

2. Goleman, D. (1995). Emotional Intelligence: Why It Can Matter More Than IQ. New York: Bantam Books.

### Layer 3: Specificity and Clarity - The Precision of Impactful Feedback

Effective feedback is like a finely-tuned instrument, providing clear, precise insights that resonate with the recipient. By offering concrete examples and actionable suggestions, feedback becomes a guiding compass, directing individuals toward targeted areas of improvement and growth.

## The Power of Being Clear and Specific

Clear and specific leaves no room for ambiguity or misinterpretation. It serves as a roadmap for improvement, enabling individuals to understand precisely what aspects of their performance or behavior require attention. By addressing specific actions, behaviors, or outcomes, feedback becomes a potent tool for change.

Imagine a graphic designer receiving feedback on a project. Instead of vague comments like "make it better," the feedback provides specific insights on color choices, font sizes, and image placement. With this clarity, the designer can confidently revise the project, knowing precisely which aspects to enhance.

Clear and specific feedback aligns with the principles of cognitive psychology, which highlights the importance of precise information in the learning process. When individuals receive well-defined feedback, it facilitates their understanding and retention of the information, leading to more effective skill development.

## Avoiding the Pitfalls of Ambiguity

Conversely, vague or ambiguous feedback can hinder growth and progress. When feedback lacks specificity, individuals struggle to grasp its intended meaning, leaving them unsure about the necessary improvements. The ambiguity can lead to frustration and confusion, impeding the potential to drive positive change.

Consider an employee receiving feedback from their manager, stating that they need to "improve communication skills." Without specific examples or context, the employee is uncertain about which aspects of their communication need attention, making it difficult to take meaningful action.

Ambiguous feedback can be demotivating, leaving individuals

feeling uncertain and disheartened. On the other hand, clear feedback provides a sense of direction and purpose, fostering motivation and commitment to improvement.

## The Precision Transformation

There is transformative power in clear and specific feedback. Feedback can support positive change by providing recipients with a roadmap for growth. Leaders and feedback providers must hone their ability to offer feedback that is not only meaningful but also actionable, empowering individuals to embark on a journey of continuous improvement.

## References:

1. Hattie, J., & Timperley, H. (2007). The Power of Feedback. Review of Educational Research, 77(1), 81-112.

2. Bandura, A. (1997). Self-Efficacy: The Exercise of Control. New York: W.H. Freeman and Company.

## Layer 4: Intent and Motive - The Heart of Feedback

Feedback is not merely about the spoken words; it carries the weight of the giver's intentions and emotions. The power of genuine care and support in feedback delivery fosters an environment of trust and receptivity, while hidden agendas or ill intentions create barriers to growth and improvement.

## The Influence of Genuine Care and Support

Feedback emanating from genuine care and support reflects the giver's desire to see the recipient succeed. When constructive feedback is correctly offered with the best interest of the individual or team in mind, it creates an atmosphere of psychological safety. Individuals are more likely to perceive feedback as a tool for their development rather than a judgment of their worth. The spirit of empathy and understanding behind feedback enhances its effectiveness and ensures it is received with an open heart.

Imagine a mentor providing feedback to a mentee on a

challenging project. The mentor prefaces the feedback by expressing their belief in the mentee's potential and emphasizing their commitment to helping them grow. Feeling valued and supported, the mentee is more receptive to the feedback, knowing it comes from a place of genuine care.

Feedback grounded in positive intent aligns with trust-building principles in interpersonal relationships. When individuals sense that feedback comes from a place of concern for their growth, it strengthens the bond between giver and recipient, fostering a collaborative and growth-oriented dynamic.

## Avoiding the Pitfalls of Hidden Agendas

On the contrary, feedback offered with hidden agendas or ill intentions can harm the recipient's perception and willingness to engage with future feedback. If individuals sense ulterior motives, such as seeking to undermine or control them, they become guarded and defensive, hindering their receptivity to feedback in general.

For instance, Jane receives feedback from her colleague, Alex, in a corporate setting after a successful project completion. The intention behind Alex's feedback is not to genuinely support Jane's growth and success but rather to create doubt or diminish her achievements. This intent creates a subtle undertone in Alex's feedback. Janes senses underlying elements of undermining and manipulation. As a result, Jane becomes cautious and hesitant to accept future feedback from Alex, wary of potential ulterior motives that could impact her career growth. This not only impacts Jane, but as the word spreads (and it will), it will disrupt the entire feedback culture of the team.

What would give Jane a reason to be suspicious? Alex may employ various tactics to undermine Jane's chances at promotion:

**Ambiguous Praise:** Alex's praise might be vague and lack specificity, leaving Jane uncertain about which aspects of her work were truly commendable. This ambiguity makes it difficult for Jane to build a strong case for her promotion when discussing her accomplishments with higher-ups.

**Highlighting Weaknesses:** Disguised within the praise, Alex may subtly highlight Jane's weaknesses or areas where she fell short without offering constructive comments. By doing so, Alex casts doubt on Jane's overall competence, making it harder for her to be considered for promotion.

**Undermining Confidence:** Through backhanded compliments or sly comparisons to other colleagues, Alex aims to erode Jane's confidence. A less confident Jane may doubt her abilities and be less assertive in advocating for her own promotion.

**Spreading Disinformation:** In more malicious scenarios, Alex might spread false information about Jane's performance to others in the company, tarnishing her reputation and credibility. This smear campaign can impact the decision-makers perception of Jane's suitability for promotion but can also find its way back to Jane.

**Claiming Credit for Jane's Work:** Alex might subtly imply or take undue credit for Jane's achievements during collaborative projects. This tactic undermines Jane's contributions, potentially leaving her efforts unnoticed by those involved in promotion decisions.

Overall, Alex's intention is not to genuinely support Jane's professional growth but rather to position herself favorably for promotion opportunities by diminishing Jane's standing within the organization. By creating an atmosphere of doubt and uncertainty around Jane's performance, Alex attempts to elevate her own chances for advancement, undermining Jane's potential for promotion.

*Know anyone like this in your organization?*

Feedback with hidden agendas can trigger a threat response as individuals perceive potential harm to their well-being. This threat can lead to heightened defensiveness and resistance, limiting the feedback's potential to foster growth. Not to mention the tension created within the team.

## The Heartbeat of Feedback

By now, we recognize that feedback carries an emotional charge that goes beyond the spoken word. Intent and motive are the heartbeat of feedback, shaping the recipient's perception and response. Leaders and feedback providers must cultivate self-awareness and empathy, ensuring their feedback is guided by authentic care and support.

By understanding the profound influence of intent and motive, we can foster a feedback culture that celebrates growth, inspires excellence, and nurtures the potential of individuals and teams.

## References:

1. Mayer, R. C., Davis, J. H., & Schoorman, F. D. (1995). An integrative model of organizational trust. Academy of Management Review, 20(3), 709-734.

2. Deci, E. L., & Ryan, R. M. (2002). Handbook of self-determination research. University of Rochester Press.

## Layer 5: Relevance and Timeliness - The Power of Contextual Alignment

Like a compass, feedback gains its full potential when it aligns with an individual's current goals and performance. Moreover, delivering feedback promptly after observing the behavior provides context, fostering more meaningful and impactful discussions.

## The Impact of Relevance

Relevant feedback is a key driver of engagement and motivation.

When feedback is tailored to an individual's specific goals and aspirations, it resonates personally, making it more likely to be internalized and acted upon.

Consider a sales representative, Bob, whose primary goal is to increase customer satisfaction. The relevant feedback provided by the manager focuses on Bob's interactions with clients, highlighting areas where he excels in customer service and offering strategies to further improve customer relationships. Tailored to Bob's aspirations, this feedback fuels his commitment to excel in his role. The Self-Determination Theory suggests that feedback that supports an individual's sense of autonomy and competence enhances their intrinsic motivation to pursue improvement.

**The Power of Timeliness**

Timely feedback carries a heightened impact due to its connection to the behavior. When feedback is provided soon after the event or performance, individuals can recall the context and specifics more vividly, enhancing the feedback's effectiveness in driving behavioral change.

Imagine a team member, Sarah, who leads a critical project. Her manager provides timely feedback immediately after the project presentation, addressing the strengths and improvement areas. The prompt feedback allows Sarah to reflect on her performance while the experience is fresh, enabling her to make necessary adjustments for future projects.

Timely feedback capitalizes on the primacy and recency effects in memory retention. The information delivered close to the observed behavior is more likely to be stored in long-term memory, aiding the learning and improvement process.

**The Synchrony of Feedback**

Synchrony of feedback is where relevance and timeliness converge to optimize impact. Aligning feedback with individuals' goals nurtures a sense of purpose, while timely delivery captures the essence of the observed behavior. Leaders and feedback providers must consider both factors to ensure their feedback has the desired effect of fostering growth and development.

### References:

1. Deci, E. L., & Ryan, R. M. (2000). The "what" and "why" of goal pursuits: Human needs and the self-determination of behavior. Psychological Inquiry, 11(4), 227-268.

2. Carpenter, S., Wilford, M., & Sahraie, A. (2013). The primacy and recency effect within the context of recognition memory. Quarterly Journal of Experimental Psychology, 66(8), 1579-1594.

## Layer 6: Frequency and Consistency - The Rhythm of Continuous Improvement

Like the steady beat of a drum, regular feedback sustains the momentum of growth and development, enabling individuals to track their progress and make continuous improvements. Conversely, infrequent feedback can create gaps in understanding and hinder the realization of untapped potential.

### The Power of Frequent Feedback

Frequent feedback establishes a continuous feedback loop that fosters a culture of improvement. When individuals receive feedback regularly, they better understand their strengths and areas for development. This ongoing exchange of insights provides a foundation for consistent growth and learning.

Consider a software developer, John, who receives regular feedback from his team lead after each sprint. The consistent feedback allows John to adapt and fine-tune his coding practices, leading to a more efficient and error-free development process. The regular feedback loop enables John to make incremental improvements over time.

Frequent feedback aligns with the principles of spaced repetition in learning and memory. Regular feedback reinforcement ensures the information remains fresh and accessible, enhancing individuals' ability to retain and apply it effectively.

## The Influence of Consistency on Behavior

Consistent feedback aligns with behavioral psychology, where repeated reinforcement of positive behaviors leads to sustainable integration. When individuals receive consistent feedback on their strengths and progress, they are likelier to continue the behaviors contributing to their success.

The combination of frequent and consistent feedback nurtures a dynamic environment of growth and learning. Leaders and feedback providers must recognize the power of this cadence, ensuring that feedback becomes an ongoing dialogue that empowers individuals to strive for excellence.

## References:

1. Cepeda, N. J., Pashler, H., Vul, E., Wixted, J. T., & Rohrer, D. (2006). Distributed practice in verbal recall tasks: A review and quantitative synthesis. Psychological Bulletin, 132(3), 354-380.

2. Skinner, B. F. (1938). The Behavior of Organisms: An Experimental Analysis. New York: Appleton-Century.

## Layer 7: Balancing Praise and Critique - The Art of Nurturing Growth

A balanced approach of praise and critique celebrates achievements and strengths while providing guidance for improvement. Like the interplay of light and shadow in a masterpiece, this equilibrium drives a healthy feedback culture that fuels motivation and encourages continuous growth.

## The Power of Genuine Praise

Praise is a powerful motivator that acknowledges individuals' efforts and accomplishments. Genuine praise fosters a sense of recognition and validation and boosts self-esteem and confidence. Recognizing and celebrating achievements contributes to a positive and supportive work environment.

Consider an employee, Mike, who successfully leads a complex project to completion. His manager acknowledges his exceptional leadership and problem-solving skills in a team meeting, praising his outstanding performance. Mike's sense of pride and achievement is heightened, inspiring him to tackle future challenges with renewed enthusiasm.

Praise aligns with the principles of intrinsic motivation, where recognition and acknowledgment of accomplishments enhance individuals' internal drive to excel and seek further growth.

## The Role of Constructive Criticism

Constructive criticism provides the necessary insights for improvement and development. By offering specific and actionable feedback on areas that require attention, individuals gain valuable guidance on enhancing their skills and performance. Emphasizing growth areas in a supportive manner helps individuals view constructive criticism as an opportunity for progress rather than a personal attack.

Imagine a marketing manager, Lisa, receiving feedback on a campaign proposal. Her supervisor highlights the campaign's strengths while offering constructive suggestions for refining the targeting strategy. The supervisor provides this feedback shortly after the proposal and offers heartfelt encouragement and helpful suggestions for refinement that should allow Lisa to provide a better deliverable. Lisa appreciates the guidance and adopts the suggestions, leading to a more effective campaign.

Constructive criticism aligns with Bandura's self-efficacy theory, where individuals' beliefs in their abilities are influenced by feedback. Individuals gain confidence in their capacity to achieve desired outcomes by providing specific guidance for improvement.

## The Harmony of Growth

Balancing praise and critique is necessary to create a harmonious feedback culture. Celebrating achievements while providing constructive guidance allows feedback to be an opportunity for growth and development. Leaders and feedback providers must master this art, ensuring their feedback nurtures a positive and empowered workforce.

## References:

1. Deci, E. L., & Ryan, R. M. (1985). Intrinsic Motivation and Self-Determination in Human Behavior. New York: Plenum.
2. Bandura, A. (1997). Self-Efficacy: The Exercise of Control. New York: W.H. Freeman and Company.

## Layer 8: Psychological Safety - The Bedrock of Trust and Growth

Psychological safety is the fertile ground upon which the seeds of trust, vulnerability, and growth take root and flourish. In an environment of psychological safety, individuals experience a profound sense of security and support, allowing them to express themselves freely and authentically. This nurturing space empowers individuals to open themselves to feedback, knowing their contributions will be met with understanding and constructive guidance rather than destructive criticism or punishment.

Armed with this assurance, team members are emboldened to step out of their comfort zones and explore uncharted territories, taking calculated risks to pursue innovative solutions and novel approaches. Psychological safety becomes the required ingredient for a culture of continuous improvement, where mistakes are seen not as failures but as pathways for learning and progress.

This vibrant ecosystem of trust and support fosters an unyielding spirit of growth, where individuals and teams thrive, unlocking their full potential and reaching new heights of excellence.

## The Foundation of Trust

Psychological safety is the bedrock of trust in any organization or team. When individuals feel safe expressing their thoughts and ideas, they are more likely to collaborate, share feedback, and engage in constructive discussions. Trust fosters an environment where feedback becomes a genuine exchange of insights rather than a source of anxiety or tension.

In a team where psychological safety prevails, members engage in regular feedback sessions, openly discussing successes and challenges. The leader fosters an atmosphere of trust and respect, encouraging everyone to share their perspectives without fear of negative consequences. As a result, team members feel valued and supported, enabling a robust feedback culture.

Psychological safety aligns with research on risk-taking behavior, showing that individuals are more willing to take calculated risks when they feel secure and supported in their environment.

## Embracing Vulnerability for Growth

This environment of safety nurtures vulnerability, allowing individuals to admit mistakes and seek help when needed. When people feel accepted and understood, they are more open to acknowledging areas where they need improvement, fostering a culture of continuous growth.

For example, in a weekly team meeting, Sarah, a dedicated and hardworking employee, musters the courage to address her recent mistake in a high-stakes project. As she takes a deep breath, she admits to the team that she misjudged a critical deadline, delaying the project's completion. In the following silence, Sarah feels a mix of nerves and vulnerability, uncertain of how her colleagues and team leader will react. However, to her relief and surprise, the team leader, Susan, responds with genuine understanding and reassurance. She acknowledges Sarah's willingness to share her mistake openly and commendably. Susan emphasizes that mistakes are not signs of failure but opportunities for learning and growth. She assures Sarah that she is not alone in making errors and that the team supports her through challenges and triumphs.

The reaction from the rest of the team mirrors that of the team leader. Rather than judgment or criticism, Sarah is met with empathy and support. Her teammates share stories of their own past mistakes, highlighting that such experiences have been turning points in their professional journeys. The team's willingness to be vulnerable about their own errors creates a safe space where learning from mistakes is valued, not condemned.

Feeling encouraged and emboldened, Sarah reflects on the feedback and guidance shared by her colleagues. She understands that her vulnerability has led to a deeper connection with the team, fostering a sense of camaraderie and mutual growth. The team meeting becomes an inspiring example of how psychological safety can transform the dynamics of a group, enabling open dialogue and fostering trust.

Over the next few weeks, Sarah takes Susan's advice to heart and embraces the opportunity to learn from her mistake. She discusses with team members, seeking their insights and suggestions for improvement. Sarah's vulnerability becomes an opening for constructive conversations and collaborative problem-solving.

As Sarah progresses with her learning journey, she receives continued support and encouragement from her team. The team leader, Susan, admires Sarah's growth and development. She recognizes the power of psychological safety in nurturing a culture of trust and growth. Susan further encourages the team to share their experiences and learnings, creating a virtuous cycle of openness, feedback, and improvement.

The positive impact of Sarah's vulnerability ripples throughout the team, transforming the way they approach challenges and opportunities. The team's feedback sessions become more constructive as everyone embraces a growth mindset. The culture of psychological safety becomes a defining trait of the team, elevating their collective performance and fostering a strong bond that transcends beyond the workplace.

## The Sanctuary for Growth

Psychological safety aligns with the principles of learning theory, where an environment of safety and acceptance enhances individuals' willingness to explore and expand their knowledge and skills. This safe environment fosters a culture of authenticity, trust, and empowerment and must be championed by leaders and feedback givers.

## References:

1. Edmondson, A. C. (1999). Psychological safety and learning behavior in work teams. Administrative Science Quarterly, 44(2), 350-383.

2. Brown, B. (2012). Daring Greatly: How the Courage to Be Vulnerable Transforms the Way We Live, Love, Parent, and Lead. New York: Avery.

## Layer 9: Reciprocity and Feedback Culture - The Ecosystem of Growth

A culture that champions open and honest communication, where feedback becomes a two-way street flowing both top-down and bottom-up, creates an ecosystem of continuous improvement and mutual support.

## The Impact of Feedback Culture

When feedback is ingrained as an integral part of the organizational DNA, team members are more likely to perceive feedback as a valuable asset, not a dreaded obligation. A robust feedback culture transcends hierarchy and empowers individuals to engage in candid conversations that drive collective progress.

Consider an innovative tech company that fosters a culture of reciprocity and feedback. Everyone from the CEO to entry-level employees actively provides and receives feedback. Employees are encouraged to share insights and ideas freely, and feedback sessions are celebrated as opportunities for growth. This vibrant ecosystem ignites a culture of continuous learning, where everyone contributes to the organization's evolution.

Feedback culture aligns with research on the role of culture in shaping individuals' perceptions and attitudes. When feedback is woven into the fabric of an organization, it shapes how individuals perceive and interpret the feedback they receive.

## The Power of Reciprocity

Reciprocity fuels the feedback loop, nurturing a sense of fairness and camaraderie. When individuals see their feedback valued and acted upon, they are motivated to reciprocate, asking for insights and support from others. This virtuous cycle fosters a climate of trust and collaboration, propelling the organization toward success. In a team where the spirit of reciprocity thrives, the culture of feedback becomes a cornerstone of their collective success. Team members actively seek opportunities to support and uplift one another through open and candid feedback exchanges.

For example, John, a seasoned and respected team member, recently presented a critical project update to the team. Sarah, a junior colleague with a fresh perspective, observes the presentation and recognizes an opportunity for improvement. Sarah summons her courage and dedication to the team's success and takes the initiative to share constructive feedback with John after the presentation. Sarah acknowledges the strengths of John's presentation but also offers insightful suggestions for enhancing the clarity of certain points and creating a stronger impact. John listens attentively to Sarah's input, recognizing the value of her perspective, and appreciates her willingness to speak up.

John, humbled by Sarah's thoughtfulness and recognizing her expertise in her area of work, seeks an opportunity to reciprocate her act of kindness and support. Sarah is currently leading a high-stakes project, and John takes the time to review her project's proposal and execution plan in detail. He gives Sarah thoughtful and encouraging feedback, offering strategies to navigate potential challenges and leverage her team's strengths.

This feedback exchange strengthens a bond for both John and Sarah as individuals and the entire team. By fostering a culture of reciprocity, the team creates an environment where trust and collaboration flourish. Team members feel empowered to share their insights and seek feedback without hesitation, knowing their contributions are valued and respected.

The impact of this culture reverberates throughout the team's dynamics. As individuals engage in reciprocal feedback, they build strong bonds, deepening their mutual understanding and appreciation for each other's strengths. Team cohesion strengthens, and collective intelligence takes center stage, fueling the team's ability to navigate challenges with resilience and creativity.

The team's overall performance elevates to new heights due to this feedback-driven culture. Communication becomes more transparent and solutions-oriented. Productivity increases and innovative ideas flow freely. As a united force, the team achieves remarkable outcomes and garners recognition for their exceptional achievements.

Beyond their immediate successes, the team's reputation attracts talent from across the organization, drawn to the culture of growth and support. As new members join the team, they are warmly welcomed into this environment of reciprocity, quickly assimilating into the collective spirit of continuous improvement.

In this team, feedback is no longer seen as an isolated event or a top-down exercise but rather as an organic and intrinsic part of their identity. The spirit of reciprocity and constructive feedback is now deeply embedded in the team's DNA, driving their journey toward sustained excellence and making them models for others to emulate.

This example exemplifies the transformative power of reciprocity in a feedback culture, where the act of giving and receiving feedback becomes a catalyst for personal and collective growth. As leaders nurture and champion this culture, they create a work environment where everyone feels valued, empowered, and inspired to reach their full potential. The team's success is a testament to reciprocity's profound impact in cultivating high-performing teams and fostering an environment of continuous excellence.

Reciprocity aligns with social exchange theory, where individuals reciprocate positive actions to build and maintain social bonds within a group.

## Nurturing an Ecosystem of Growth

Leaders play a pivotal role in cultivating this culture of empowerment and growth when they understand that feedback is not about criticism or fault-finding but recognizing and developing everyone's unique potential. By ensuring everyone is trained on constructive criticism methods and setting the tone and example, leaders create an environment where feedback is not feared but welcomed as a workshop for improvement and learning.

A leader's ability to actively listen and respond empathetically to feedback is key to cultivating an open and supportive culture. When employees know their voices are heard and their perspectives are respected, they feel more invested in the organization's success. Leaders who take the time to engage in meaningful feedback conversations demonstrate their commitment to the growth and development of their team members. They recognize that mistakes are an inevitable part of progress and encourage their teams to embrace challenges, take risks, and push boundaries.

Through the lens of reciprocity, organizations create a virtuous cycle of improvement. When individuals experience the benefits of constructive feedback and support, they are inspired to reciprocate the same level of commitment to their colleagues. This spirit of reciprocity strengthens teamwork and enhances the overall organizational culture. In this upward spiral of improvement, every individual plays a crucial role in contributing to the shared journey of success. The culture of feedback and learning becomes a collective endeavor where everyone is invested in the organization's growth and success. As employees witness the positive impact of their feedback on their colleagues, they become more eager to share insights and offer support. This culture of empowerment and collective improvement propels the organization towards greater success.

### References:

1. Hui, C., Lee, C., & Rousseau, D. M. (2004). Psychological contract and organizational citizenship behavior in China: Investigating generalizability and instrumentality. Journal of Applied Psychology, 89(2), 311-321.

2. Greenberg, J. (1986). Determinants of perceived fairness of performance evaluations. Journal of Applied Psychology, 71(2), 340-342.

## Layer 10: Growth Mindset and Attitude - The Stimulant for Transformation

The recipient's growth mindset and attitude toward feedback become the key differentiators in how individuals embrace and respond to feedback. A growth mindset empowers individuals to view constructive feedback as an invaluable opportunity for learning and growth, while a fixed mindset may lead them to perceive feedback as a judgment of their inherent abilities.

## The Power of a Growth Mindset

Individuals with a growth mindset believe their abilities and intelligence can be developed through effort, perseverance, and learning from mistakes. They embrace challenges and see setbacks as scenic overlooks in the drive toward mastery. When feedback is presented to someone with a growth mindset, they approach it with curiosity and eagerness, viewing it as a chance to enhance their skills and advance their potential.

Consider Emma, an ambitious project manager with a growth mindset who receives feedback on her recent project. As a highly driven individual, Emma always seeks growth and improvement opportunities. When her team and stakeholders provide feedback, highlighting areas where she could have enhanced her communication with the team, Emma's response is one of receptiveness and enthusiasm.

Instead of feeling defensive or discouraged by the feedback, Emma views it as a valuable opportunity to enhance her leadership skills. She understands that effective communication is crucial for successful project management and collaboration. With a growth mindset as her guiding compass, Emma sets out on a journey of self-improvement, determined to enhance her communication abilities.

Firstly, Emma proactively seeks advice and insights from her peers and mentors. She values their expertise and recognizes the collective knowledge available to her. Through candid conversations and mentorship sessions, Emma gains valuable insights and practical tips to enhance her communication style.

Moreover, Emma takes a proactive step in her pursuit of growth by enrolling in communication workshops and seminars. By immersing herself in these learning opportunities, she gains a deeper understanding of effective communication techniques, active listening, and the art of delivering clear and impactful messages. Armed with this newfound knowledge, Emma is eager to apply these strategies to her leadership approach.

Emma's growth mindset fuels her determination to incorporate new strategies into her leadership style. She actively experiments with different communication techniques, seeking feedback along the way to gauge their effectiveness. Emma fosters a transparent and collaborative work environment by applying these strategies in real-world scenarios.

As a result of her commitment to growth, Emma's leadership skills undergo a remarkable transformation. Her team members notice a positive shift in communication dynamics, with clearer instructions, active engagement, and a heightened sense of camaraderie. Stakeholders also acknowledge the improvement, noting the increased efficiency and alignment within the project.

Beyond the immediate project's success, Emma's growth mindset has a lasting impact on her team and the organization. Her receptiveness to feedback inspires her team members to be more open to receiving feedback themselves, fostering a culture of continuous improvement and learning.

As her leadership abilities continue to evolve, Emma becomes a role model for others within the organization. She shares her growth journey and the value she places on feedback, encouraging her colleagues to embrace challenges and seek opportunities for growth. Her enthusiasm for personal development creates a wave throughout the organization, igniting a collective desire for excellence.

Emma's growth mindset ultimately enhances her leadership skills and elevates her team and organization's overall performance and culture. Her story serves as a testament to the incredible potential that lies within a growth mindset—a mindset that turns feedback into a catalyst for growth and transformation, empowering individuals like Emma to continuously strive for excellence and inspire those around them.

A growth mindset aligns with the research of Carol Dweck, highlighting the impact of beliefs on individuals' motivation, learning, and achievement. Dweck's studies show that a growth mindset is a catalyst for resilience and continuous improvement.

## Navigating a Fixed Mindset

On the other hand, individuals with a fixed mindset believe that their abilities are fixed traits, and they avoid challenges that might expose their limitations. Feedback in any form can threaten them, as it may reinforce the belief that they lack innate skills or talents. As a result, they may become defensive or resistant to feedback, hindering their growth and development.

For example, Alex, a talented graphic designer with a fixed mindset, finds himself at a crossroads when he receives feedback on a recent project. Despite his skill and creativity, he is confronted with constructive criticism that points out areas for improvement in his design choices. As the feedback is presented to him, Alex's initial reaction is one of defensiveness and dismissal.

Alex's fixed mindset becomes a barrier to accepting and internalizing the feedback because he feels his artistic abilities are being questioned. In his mind, he perceives the feedback as a personal attack on his talents rather than an opportunity for growth. The fear of being exposed as lacking in artistic prowess threatens his self-image as a designer, leading him to resist the feedback rather than embrace it as a valuable insight.

The consequences of this fixed mindset on Alex's growth and development are profound. As he avoids seeking feedback in the future, he inadvertently deprives himself of the valuable learning opportunities that come with constructive criticism. By shielding himself from feedback, he remains stuck in his current skill level and limits his potential for improvement.

Additionally, Alex's hesitance to take on challenging projects stems from a fear of potential failure. Remember the section on psychological safety? He becomes reluctant to step out of his comfort zone and explore new creative territories as he worries about the potential for further criticism and validation of his insecurities. As a result, his growth as a designer becomes stunted, and he misses out on the chance to push his boundaries and discover new dimensions of his talent.

This scenario illustrates the profound impact of a fixed mindset on an individual's response to feedback and, subsequently, on their growth trajectory. Alex's fixed mindset becomes a self-fulfilling prophecy, as his reluctance to embrace feedback perpetuates a cycle of stagnation, hindering his evolution as a graphic designer.

However, with the right support and encouragement, Alex has the potential to break free from the confines of a fixed mindset. By cultivating a growth mindset, he can transform his perception of feedback from a threat to an opportunity. Through a growth mindset lens, Alex can use feedback to hone his craft and reach new heights in his creative journey.

Leaders and mentors play a critical role in nurturing a growth mindset culture. By providing a safe and supportive environment for feedback, they can help individuals like Alex overcome their defensiveness and foster a culture of continuous learning and improvement.

With time and guidance, Alex may gradually embrace feedback as an essential part of his growth as a designer. As he recognizes that even the most accomplished artists continue to learn and evolve, he becomes more open to seeking feedback and exploring new challenges. As a result, Alex's growth eventually flourishes, and he becomes a testament to the transformative power of a growth mindset in unlocking one's full potential.

## The Fixed Mindset Trap

The concept of a fixed mindset, also explored by Carol Dweck, underscores the impact of beliefs on the individuals' response to feedback and their willingness to embrace challenges and opportunities for growth.

Organizations prioritizing a growth mindset culture encourage employees to see feedback as an integral part of their development journey. Leaders must play a crucial role in nurturing this mindset by promoting a learning-oriented environment, where mistakes are embraced as opportunities for growth and feedback is viewed as a gateway to excellence. Environments that cultivate a growth mindset culture unlock the transformative power of feedback, inspiring individuals to embrace challenges, learn from experiences, and continuously elevate their performance. As leaders foster this mindset, they lay the foundation for a dynamic and resilient workforce, driving the organization toward a future of excellence and achievement.

### References:

1. Dweck, C. S. (2006). Mindset: The New Psychology of Success. New York: Random House.
2. Mueller, C. M., & Dweck, C. S. (1998). Praise for intelligence can undermine children's motivation and performance. Journal of Personality and Social Psychology, 75(1), 33-52.

Having delved into the intricate nature of feedback, we have surfaced both its potential for empowerment and the danger of it causing harm. We've illuminated the difference between feedback that builds and criticism that breaks, emphasizing the pivotal role of delivery and reception in determining the outcome.

With the help of examples and insights from the realm of psychology, we've seen the transformative power of specific, transparent, and timely feedback. Moreover, we've recognized that a harmonious environment where praise and critique coexist is essential for nurturing a culture where feedback is valued and heeded.

These pages showed that feedback isn't merely a passing remark or a simple exchange. It's a powerful conduit for personal and organizational growth, steering us toward constant betterment. In the next chapter, we'll talk about why thinking that all feedback is a gift creates a minefield that is just as powerful to stop personal growth and destroy teams.

# CHAPTER 2: THE DARK SIDE OF GIFTED FEEDBACK

Now we will shine a light on the dark side of feedback as a gift. We will uncover how the one-size-fits-all approach to feedback creates an environment of forced positivity, stifling honest conversations and hindering authentic growth. We will also address the power dynamics at play in feedback exchanges, acknowledging that the perceived "gift" may carry unintended power imbalances that can skew its impact.

**The Forced Positivity Trap**

The allure of the "gifted" feedback approach lies in its intention to be supportive and uplifting. However, this approach can become a double-edged sword, trapping individuals and organizations in the web of forced positivity. To protect recipients from potential discomfort, feedback providers may opt to withhold constructive criticism, favoring praise and positive reinforcement. While the intentions behind this approach are well-meaning, it inadvertently prevents individuals from receiving the valuable insights they need to grow and improve.

Amidst the abundance of praise, individuals may find themselves swimming in accolades for their achievements. While recognition is undoubtedly important for boosting morale, an overdose of praise without honest feedback can create a false sense of accomplishment and hinder further progress. When feedback providers avoid addressing developmental areas, it comes at a high cost – the missed opportunities for growth. Unaddressed weaknesses can persist, preventing individuals from honing their skills and realizing their potential. The result is a stagnant environment where progress is stifled, and potential remains untapped.

Organizations must cultivate a culture of candid feedback to break free from the forced positivity trap. When delivered with empathy and respect, constructive criticism can be a powerful motivation for improvement and innovation. By embracing honest conversations, individuals can identify their growth opportunities and take meaningful steps toward advancement. The key lies in striking a balance between praise and constructive criticism. Feedback providers must recognize their complementary nature rather than viewing them as opposing forces. Celebrating accomplishments while acknowledging areas for improvement creates a culture of continuous growth and development.

Feedback providers must be empowered to deliver constructive criticism with confidence and tact. At the same time, feedback receivers should be encouraged to view such feedback not as a gift but rather as an opportunity to review valuable data that may help them improve in their journey toward excellence.

### The Illusion of Growth: Surface-Level Feedback

Surface-level feedback may provide a fleeting sense of achievement but lacks the substance necessary for sustainable growth. The momentary ego boost from vague praise or sugar-coated compliments can create an illusion of progress, leading individuals to believe they excel when genuine improvement is lacking.

Without the depth and specificity of constructive feedback, individuals may find it challenging to gauge their true performance. The absence of actionable insights leaves them in the dark about areas where they could excel with further development. As a result, their potential for growth remains untapped, hidden beneath the guise of surface-level accolades.

The illusion of growth can breed complacency. When individuals perceive themselves as achieving their best, they may resist seeking further improvement. This complacency stifles ambition and innovation, preventing individuals from reaching new heights in their personal and professional endeavors. To break free from the illusion of growth, individuals must embrace constructive feedback as a powerful magnet for genuine progress. Specific and actionable feedback shines a light on areas that need improvement, propelling individuals forward in their growth journey.

## Unraveling Power Dynamics: The Impact of Giver and Receiver

In the intricate dance of feedback exchanges, power dynamics quietly influence the dynamics between the giver and receiver, significantly shaping the impact of feedback and the authenticity of growth. By examining the incorrect notion that all feedback is a gift, we can uncover the hidden forces at play and work towards a more empowering and equitable feedback culture.

## The Gift-Giver as an Authority Figure

Feedback interactions often involve a giver who assumes the role of an authority figure or evaluator. Whether it's a manager, supervisor, or an experienced colleague, their position and perceived expertise elevate their status in the feedback exchange. This dynamic can create an implicit power imbalance, where the receiver may hesitate to challenge or question the feedback, fearing potential repercussions.

In this power dynamic, the receiver may find themselves vulnerable, expected to accept the feedback unquestioningly. The fear of appearing ungrateful or disrespectful can deter individuals from engaging in candid and open conversations about their performance. As a result, honest discussions about developmental areas may be withheld, limiting opportunities for genuine growth.

When feedback is viewed as a gift, the fear of challenging its validity can hinder growth. After all, you wouldn't normally reject a gift, would you? Therefore, you may feel compelled to accept feedback without expressing your thoughts or seeking clarification. This fear-based hesitation stifles open communication, limiting the exchange of valuable insights that could lead to significant improvements.

## A Superficial Approach to Feedback

In environments where feedback is treated as a one-way transaction, superficial compliments may become the norm. Without candid discussions about areas for improvement, the feedback provided may lack the depth needed to guide individuals on their growth journey. As a result, developing essential skills and competencies could be stunted, preventing individuals from reaching their true potential.

## Empowering Authentic Growth

Organizations must address and dismantle the power dynamics inherent in traditional feedback exchanges to foster authentic growth. Here are some strategies to empower both givers and receivers of feedback:

Leaders and managers can create an environment where open dialogue about feedback is actively encouraged. By fostering a culture of psychological safety, individuals will feel more comfortable sharing their perspectives, leading to richer and more constructive feedback discussions.

Feedback should be seen as a two-way conversation rather than a top-down evaluation. Both givers and receivers should actively listen and be open to seeking mutual understanding and growth.

Promoting a growth mindset encourages individuals to see feedback as an opportunity for learning and improvement rather than a judgment of their abilities. Embracing this mindset empowers individuals to proactively seek feedback and continuously strive for personal and professional growth.

Unraveling the power dynamics in feedback exchanges is essential for fostering authentic growth and development. By recognizing the influence of the feedback giver and empowering the vulnerable receiver, organizations can create a feedback culture that encourages open dialogue and embraces growth mindsets.

**Nurturing Psychological Safety: Empowering the Receiver**

In pursuing a feedback culture that transcends the limitations of power dynamics, organizations must prioritize cultivating psychological safety. Leaders must foster an environment where individuals feel secure to express themselves, take risks, and ask questions without fear of retribution or judgment. Only then can organizations empower feedback receivers to embrace feedback as a powerful tool for growth.

Psychological safety is required for a healthy feedback process. When individuals feel safe and supported, they are more receptive to receiving feedback with an open mind and a growth-oriented attitude. Individuals are encouraged to share their challenges and seek clarification without hesitation in a psychologically safe environment. This fosters authentic and meaningful feedback conversations, where both the giver and receiver engage in open dialogue and mutual understanding. Such conversations transcend the mere exchange of information and become transformative experiences that lead to genuine growth and development.

Leaders play a pivotal role in nurturing psychological safety within feedback processes. By leading by example, they showcase their willingness to receive feedback and demonstrate a growth mindset. When leaders embrace feedback as a valuable tool for their own development, it sets the tone for the entire organization to follow suit.

## Training is a Requirement

Feedback training and coaching are essential to create a safe environment and empower individuals to both provide and receive feedback effectively. Givers can diminish the power dynamics inherent in traditional feedback exchanges by focusing on specific behaviors and outcomes rather than personal traits. This shift in focus emphasizes actionable and developmental feedback, where the goal is mutual growth and shared success.

Organizations should embrace a growth culture that celebrates learning and development. Normalizing feedback as an integral part of continuous improvement will encourage individuals to seek and offer feedback, leading to a more dynamic and constructive feedback ecosystem.

## Embracing Authentic Growth: A New Perspective

To unlock the true potential of feedback, we must redefine the concept of gifting feedback. Authentic growth requires a balance between celebration and critique, empowering individuals to confront challenges and seize opportunities for improvement.

Feedback, a multifaceted interaction, requires the active participation of both the giver and the receiver. While much emphasis is placed on how feedback should be delivered, the receiver's role in the process is equally significant. In this next chapter, we'll embark on a journey to explore the challenges faced by those receiving feedback.

# CHAPTER 3: THE FEEDBACK RECEIVER'S DILEMMA

Feedback is not solely the giver's responsibility; the receiver plays a crucial role in the process. There are several challenges those receiving feedback face, such as the emotional toll of feedback, the fear of judgment, and the burden of accepting every piece of feedback, especially in the feedback is a gift environment. Through this understanding, we aim to empower feedback receivers to navigate the process more effectively and find constructive meaning in feedback.

For many feedback receivers, the process can be an emotional rollercoaster. Positive feedback may elicit feelings of pride and validation, while constructive criticism can lead to self-doubt and insecurity. The emotional turmoil accompanying feedback can be overwhelming, making it challenging to maintain a balanced perspective.

Understanding these emotional responses is essential to navigating the feedback landscape effectively. By recognizing that emotions are a natural part of the feedback journey, individuals can develop resilience and emotional intelligence, transforming emotional turbulence into an opportunity for self-reflection and growth.

## The Fear of Judgment: An Invisible Barrier

One of the most significant dilemmas feedback receivers face is the fear of judgment. The perception of feedback as a gift can intensify this fear, making individuals hesitant to accept feedback openly. The desire to be perceived positively and avoid judgment may lead some to mask their vulnerabilities or downplay areas for improvement.

Overcoming the fear of judgment requires a shift in perspective. Feedback is not an indictment of one's worth but an opportunity for growth and learning. By embracing a growth mindset, feedback receivers can approach feedback as a valuable tool for development rather than a judgment of their capabilities.

In a culture that glorifies feedback as a gift, the burden of acceptance can weigh heavily on feedback receivers. Feeling obliged to accept every piece of feedback without question, individuals may lose their sense of autonomy and personal agency.

Empowering feedback receivers involves understanding that they have the right to discern and evaluate feedback for its relevance and validity. *Not every piece of feedback is equally valuable*, and receivers should feel confident in filtering feedback to derive constructive insights that align with their growth goals.

**Empowering Feedback Receivers**

In the feedback exchange, the receiver's role is equally critical as that of the giver. By recognizing the multifaceted nature of emotions and addressing the fear of judgment that often looms, feedback receivers can unlock their true growth and improvement potential.

Feedback elicits a range of emotions, from pride and validation to self-doubt and uncertainty. Understanding these emotional responses is pivotal to harnessing the power of feedback effectively. Rather than viewing emotions as obstacles, feedback receivers can embrace them as opportunities for self-reflection and growth. By acknowledging and processing these feelings, feedback receivers can transform emotional turbulence into a driving force for positive change.

**Tools and Techniques for Effective Feedback Reception**

Receiving feedback effectively is an art that can be cultivated through practice and mindful approaches. From active listening and seeking clarification to filtering feedback based on relevance and credibility, there are techniques that equip feedback receivers to derive valuable insights from every feedback encounter.

### Feedback as a Two-Way Conversation

Feedback should never be one-sided; it is always a two-way conversation between the giver and receiver. Creating a feedback culture that encourages open dialogue and shared learning is critical. By actively engaging in the feedback process, feedback receivers collaborate in their own growth journey.

Embracing feedback as a shared responsibility enhances the culture of continuous improvement and mutual support within teams and organizations.

### Cultivating a Growth Mindset

You have seen and will continue to see this concept throughout this book. A growth mindset lies at the heart of constructive feedback reception. Embracing the belief that abilities and intelligence can be developed through dedication, hard work, and continuous improvement, receivers can see feedback as a means of unlocking their potential. Instead of perceiving feedback as a fixed judgment, they view it as an opportunity to learn, adapt, and grow.

### Active Listening and Open Dialogue

The feedback receiver's journey begins with active listening. Being fully present and attentive during feedback sessions lets receivers genuinely grasp the giver's perspective. Engaging in open dialogue fosters understanding and trust, creating an environment where both parties can exchange insights and collaborate toward improvement.

### Seeking Clarification

To extract valuable insights from feedback, receivers should not hesitate to seek clarification. If a piece of feedback is unclear or vague, asking specific questions to understand the context and underlying intentions can enhance the feedback's relevance and usefulness. Unfortunately, the opportunity for real dialog is missed when either the giver or receiver (or both) are unfamiliar with how to participate in constructive feedback. The opportunity becomes awkward and turns into either a drive-by "great job" comment with no meaningful insights or takes a negative turn into nothing but criticism about what went wrong. In both cases, there is little growth opportunity for the receiver.

### Embracing Feedback Filters

Not all feedback will align with the feedback receiver's growth goals or values. Empowering feedback receivers involves understanding that they have the agency to filter feedback based on its relevance and credibility. Feedback receivers can distinguish between constructive criticism that aligns with their aspirations and feedback that may not contribute significantly to their development.

### Constructive Action and Growth Plans

Constructive feedback reception goes beyond mere acceptance; it involves taking actionable steps toward improvement. Feedback receivers should develop growth plans that outline tangible objectives and actions to address the identified areas for development. Proactively seeking opportunities for learning and skill enhancement solidifies the transformative power of feedback.

### Embracing a Feedback Community

Feedback receivers can find strength and support in forming a feedback community. Engaging in peer-to-peer feedback exchanges and seeking mentorship from experienced colleagues create a mutual growth and learning culture. Collaborative feedback communities provide a safe space for individuals to share insights, seek advice, and celebrate collective achievements.

## Finding Constructive Meaning in Feedback

Ultimately, the feedback receiver's dilemma presents an opportunity for growth and self-discovery. By embracing the challenges and complexities of feedback, individuals can find constructive meaning in every piece of feedback received. Through introspection, open dialogue, and a growth mindset, feedback receivers can transform the feedback journey into a transformative personal and professional development process.

# CHAPTER 4: CRAFTING FEEDBACK FOR GROWTH - NURTURING THE SEEDS OF DEVELOPMENT

Feedback can hold transformative power when it is thoughtfully crafted to inspire growth and foster development. But it must be delivered with precision and empathy. Feedback should be tailored to be specific, actionable, and sensitive to the individual's unique context. By mastering the craft of feedback delivery, leaders can sow the seeds of positive change and create an environment where feedback leads to continuous improvement.

**The Art of Precision: Specific and Actionable Feedback**

Effective feedback leaves no room for ambiguity; it is a laser-focused beam that pinpoints areas for improvement and highlights strengths. Instead of offering vague compliments or generalizations, feedback givers must learn to identify behaviors, actions, and outcomes that require attention. By providing specific guidance and outlining actionable steps, feedback becomes a roadmap for progress, propelling individuals toward their full potential.

In the realm of effective feedback, crafting specific and actionable feedback is an indispensable skill that drives meaningful growth and development. Consider the following examples that highlight its transformative impact:

**Illuminating Areas for Improvement**

During a team meeting, a project manager provides specific and actionable feedback to a team member on their recent report. The project manager praises the thorough research but points out that the executive summary could be more concise and focused. Additionally, the project manager offers concrete examples of how the team member can improve the overall structure and flow of the report. This precise feedback empowers the team member to make targeted adjustments, resulting in a more impactful and cohesive document.

## Bridging the Gap Between Expectations and Performance

A supervisor outlines clear performance expectations for a sales representative in a performance review. The supervisor then provides specific feedback on the representative's sales approach, identifying the strengths and offering suggestions on effectively tailoring pitches to address customer objections. By providing specific guidance, the supervisor enables the sales representative to align their performance more closely with the company's goals, fostering increased sales success.

## Promoting Growth Mindset

A coach provides specific feedback to a young athlete after a game. The coach praises the athlete's dedication to training and improvement and provides specific pointers on refining their technique for better results. The coach recommends specific drills for the athlete to work on outside practice. By offering actionable suggestions for improvement, the coach instills a growth mindset in the athlete, motivating them to view challenges as opportunities for progress and to persistently pursue excellence.

## Empowering Ownership and Accountability

In a team setting, team members provide specific feedback to each other during regular peer evaluations. Instead of simply stating vague opinions, team members offer explicit examples of when their peers demonstrated effective collaboration or exceptional problem-solving skills. This specific feedback empowers the peers to take ownership of their strengths and holds them accountable for their growth areas.

### Enhancing Communication and Understanding

A supervisor engages in a one-on-one feedback session with an employee who recently gave a presentation. The supervisor comments on the employee's body language and vocal tone observed during the presentation and provides suggestions to appear more in charge of the material. By providing concrete examples, the supervisor ensures that the feedback is clear and easily understood, enabling the employee to make immediate adjustments for more impactful future presentations.

The art of crafting specific and actionable feedback is a powerful tool for nurturing growth and development. In the examples, we can see how this type of feedback illuminates areas for improvement, recognizes and reinforces strengths, and bridges the gap between expectations and performance. Furthermore, we see how it promotes a growth mindset, empowers ownership and accountability, and enhances communication between feedback givers and receivers.

### Empathy and Sensitivity: Understanding the Receiver's Context

In the intricate art of feedback delivery, true mastery goes beyond mere words; it involves a profound understanding of the receiver's individual context and emotions. We must recognize that each individual's unique experiences and challenges profoundly shape how they perceive and respond to feedback.

### The Significance of Empathy

Feedback givers must step into the receiver's shoes to understand their thoughts, emotions, and perspectives. By empathizing with the receiver's feelings and experiences, givers can tailor their feedback to resonate with their unique circumstances.

Feedback delivered with empathy fosters psychological safety within the feedback environment. When individuals sense that their feelings and experiences are acknowledged and respected, they are more likely to embrace feedback with an open heart and mind. This sense of safety creates a fertile ground for authentic growth and development.

Sensitivity complements empathy, recognizing that everyone's experiences and challenges are diverse and multifaceted. Feedback givers approach their task with care and consideration, mindful of how their words may impact the receiver's emotions. This level of sensitivity ensures that feedback is delivered with utmost compassion, nurturing a sense of trust and understanding.

Understanding the receiver's context allows feedback givers to tailor their messages effectively. Each individual's growth journey is unique; feedback must reflect this diversity. By acknowledging the receiver's personal circumstances, strengths, and areas for improvement, feedback becomes a powerful tool for growth.

Empathy and sensitivity together enable feedback givers to balance constructive criticism and support. While highlighting areas for improvement, givers do so with kindness and encouragement, inspiring receivers to embrace challenges and view feedback as an opportunity for growth.

Feedback conversations may evoke emotional responses, both positive and negative. Givers who approach feedback with empathy and sensitivity are better equipped to navigate these emotions with grace and understanding. This skill ensures that even challenging feedback exchanges are conducted with respect and care.

Empathy and sensitivity are critical for a compassionate approach to feedback. Feedback givers can create a nurturing and empowering environment by understanding and respecting the receiver's context and emotions. As you continue exploring the art of feedback, remember the profound impact of empathy and sensitivity on the feedback experience. Constantly cultivate a culture that celebrates empathy, fosters growth, and elevates the potential of every individual and team.

## Recognizing Individual Learning Styles

Recognizing individuals' diverse learning styles and preferences is paramount in the dynamic world of feedback conversations. There is a profound significance in tailoring feedback delivery to suit different learning modalities, such as visual, auditory, and kinesthetic learners.

Learning styles vary among individuals, and feedback givers must grasp the nuances of each modality. Visual learners thrive through visual aids like charts and graphs, while auditory learners absorb information through verbal communication. On the other hand, kinesthetic learners prefer a hands-on approach, engaging in physical activities to grasp concepts effectively.

By adapting feedback to align with the receiver's learning style, givers create an environment conducive to optimal internalization. When feedback is delivered in a manner that resonates with the receiver's preferred learning modality, it becomes more accessible and digestible. As a result, receivers can absorb the insights more deeply, making the feedback a truly personalized and impactful experience.

Personalized feedback fosters a deeper connection between the giver's guidance and the receiver's growth journey. Givers who consider the receiver's learning style demonstrate profound care and understanding, instilling confidence and trust in the feedback process. This strengthened connection empowers the receiver to embark on their growth journey enthusiastically and determined.

Customizing feedback requires a keen sense of observation and empathy. Givers should observe how the receiver naturally processes information and adapt their delivery accordingly. This art of customization elevates the impact of feedback, making it a transformative and valuable tool for growth.

## The Art of Constructive Criticism

The difference between feedback and constructive criticism is the core of why feedback is not a gift and why I, as supreme ruler of all management things, hereby declare that the mantra should be removed from all training materials. Now while the scribes are busy editing all existing management training materials that are out in the verse, let's discuss the difference between Constructive Criticism and Feedback.

These terms are often used interchangeably but have subtle and powerful differences. Here's a breakdown of the distinctions between them:

**Constructive Criticism:** It specifically pertains to pointing out areas that need improvement but in a way that offers solutions or alternative approaches. Its primary goal is to help someone improve in a particular area or correct specific behaviors, mistakes, or decisions. The delivery is usually more structured, it points out what isn't working but also suggests ways to make it better.

Examples:

"Your report is quite comprehensive, but it might be more impactful if you added some visual aids to illustrate the data."

"Your presentation style is engaging, but speaking a bit slower might help the audience follow you better."

**Feedback:** Feedback is a broader term encompassing positive and negative observations. It can be related to what's working well (positive feedback) or what isn't (negative feedback). Feedback provides information about someone's performance, behavior, or output. While it can be used for improvement, it can also be used to reinforce good behavior or to simply provide information without necessarily seeking change. The delivery can be formal (like in performance reviews) and informal (like day-to-day interactions).

Examples:

"You did a great job leading today's meeting."

"I saw your presentation to the client yesterday, ouch, that didn't go well at all, did it – better luck next time."

In the feedback is a gift modality, drive-by comments like the last example become too common. This does more harm than good. This is why feedback is not a gift, it is a minefield. It is a powerful resource that can do great good but also do great harm and must be given much consideration by both the giver and receiver.

All constructive criticism can be considered feedback, but not all feedback is constructive criticism. Constructive criticism is specifically geared towards improvement by offering solutions, while feedback can be a simple observation, whether positive or negative, about someone's performance or behavior.

Constructive criticism is a potent yet often misunderstood aspect. Constructive criticism possesses immense potential to drive positive change when delivered skillfully. The essence of constructive criticism lies in its focus on behaviors and outcomes, not personal traits. Feedback givers understand that constructive criticism addresses specific actions or performance areas that warrant improvement. This targeted approach shifts the focus away from personal characteristics, avoiding feelings of shame or blame.

Constructive criticism becomes a powerful growth vehicle when framed with empathy and respect. Givers must take care to deliver feedback in a manner that inspires change without diminishing the receiver's self-worth. The true transformative potential of constructive criticism is unleashed when individuals feel empowered to act upon it positively. Feedback givers encourage receivers to view constructive criticism as an opportunity for learning and development. By offering actionable steps for improvement, givers empower receivers to embark on a journey of continuous growth.

Delivering constructive criticism requires a delicate balance between offering guidance and being overly critical. Givers approach the task with mindfulness, recognizing the emotional impact of their words. By striking the right balance, feedback givers cultivate an environment where receivers are receptive to feedback and embrace change willingly.

Constructive criticism plays a central role in fostering a growth-oriented culture within organizations. Leaders who master the art of delivering constructive criticism set an example for others to follow. In a culture that embraces constructive feedback, individuals feel motivated to seek improvement and strive for excellence.

The art of providing constructive criticism transforms feedback dynamics from a daunting experience to an opportunity for growth. Feedback recipients no longer shy away from criticism; instead, they embrace it as an essential step in their journey toward personal and professional development.

### Fostering a Feedback Culture

Beyond individual feedback exchanges, crafting feedback for growth fosters a feedback culture within teams and organizations. By embracing the art of feedback delivery, leaders can cultivate an environment where feedback is viewed as a continuous learning opportunity and a collective responsibility.

Feedback becomes a language of growth and support, where team members engage in candid conversations to elevate their collective performance. A feedback culture is born, driving innovation, encouraging collaboration, and propelling the organization toward excellence.

# CHAPTER 5: THE ROLE OF PSYCHOLOGICAL SAFETY

In the intricate web of feedback dynamics, psychological safety emerges as a foundational element that enables the transformative potential of feedback to breathe. So, what exactly is it? In short, it's a feeling or belief that you can be open and honest in expressing ideas and concerns and that you can discuss successes and mistakes, both yours and others, without negative consequences.

It is not just a superficial layer of politeness or professionalism. I've been in corporate environments where the culture was very professional and polite, and little progress could be made. Why? Everyone was afraid to speak up and share their thoughts and feedback. Pointing out a negative was considered rude. Conversations were always positive, she's a rock star, he's a rock star, you knocked that out of the park, even when the results weren't always the best. That's not psychological safety but rather an enforced brand of niceness.

How do you cultivate a psychologically safe feedback culture that truly empowers individuals? Without this nurturing environment, feedback remains a hollow gift, lacking the transformative essence it holds within.

**Embracing Vulnerability and Trust: Cultivating a Safe Haven for Authentic Expression**

Psychological safety is paramount for promoting open dialogue and vulnerability. When individuals feel secure, they're more willing to share their feelings, concerns, and ideas without the apprehension of judgment. This environment fosters authenticity and paves the way for meaningful feedback exchanges.

In an environment rooted in trust, vulnerability isn't viewed as a weakness. Instead, it's appreciated as a genuine expression of one's experiences and challenges. Those receiving feedback feel valued and understood, rather than being judged for their perceived shortcomings. They are encouraged to share their aspirations and concerns, confident that they'll be met with empathy.

This foundation of trust makes feedback not just about pointing out areas of improvement, but also about supporting growth and development. Both feedback givers and recipients understand their roles in this dynamic, acknowledging the potential of their interactions to inspire positive change.

**Empowering the Givers of Feedback**

The benefits of psychological safety are not exclusive to those receiving feedback; they also profoundly affect those giving it. When feedback providers feel secure and understood, they move away from overly critical judgments and embrace a more compassionate and constructive approach. Aware of the impact their words can have, they strive to provide feedback that is both meaningful and motivating.

This atmosphere of mutual respect and trust enhances feedback conversations. It turns them into productive discussions, where both parties recognize and appreciate their respective roles and contributions. The giver offers constructive insights, and the recipient, in turn, welcomes the opportunity for growth.

When psychological safety is prevalent within an organization, it transforms the communication landscape. People engage more openly, relationships strengthen, and common goals become clearer. This environment fuels creativity, innovation, and collaboration, driving collective progress.

In this culture, the seeds of growth are sown, watered by empathy, and nurtured by understanding. It fosters a shared commitment to learning and mutual support, setting off a cycle of continuous improvement and development. Embracing this ethos of psychological safety, we pave the way for a feedback-driven environment where every voice matters and the journey towards growth becomes a united effort.

### Strategies for Building Psychological Safety: Nurturing a Haven of Trust and Growth

Within the labyrinth of organizational dynamics lies a treasure trove of practical strategies for building psychological safety – the elixir that unleashes the true potential of feedback. Let's unveil a treasure map of actionable steps that leaders can take to foster an environment where trust thrives, growth blooms, and feedback becomes a transformative force.

### Lead with Vulnerability and Authenticity

Leaders hold the key to unlocking psychological safety within their teams. By embracing vulnerability and authenticity themselves, leaders set the stage for others to do the same. Transparently sharing their challenges, learnings, and growth aspirations, leaders create a safe space for team members to feel comfortable in their imperfections and open up about their journeys. What are other ways leaders unlock psychological safety?

### Encourage Curiosity and Learning

In a psychologically safe environment, curiosity reigns supreme. Leaders must encourage a culture where questions are expected and curiosity is nurtured. They must emphasize learning over perfection, valuing the process of growth and exploration as this fosters an atmosphere where team members feel empowered to seek feedback as a means to enhance their knowledge and skills rather than fearing it as a verdict on their abilities.

For instance, a team member reports that their latest efforts did not produce the expected results. As a result, the team is going to miss an important deadline for the project. A curious manager's first question might be, "How did this happen," but a manager focused on creating a psychologically safe environment might first ask, "What did we learn?".

## Embrace Diverse Perspectives

Leaders should champion diversity and actively seek out diverse perspectives to enrich the feedback landscape. They create opportunities for individuals from different backgrounds to share their insights, paving the way for a mosaic of viewpoints that fosters deeper understanding and empathy.

## Create a Fail-Friendly Culture

Leaders must also cultivate a fail-friendly culture, where mistakes are not stigmatized but embraced as opportunities for improvement. By doing this, leaders instill resilience and the courage to experiment and learn from setbacks by destigmatizing failure and encouraging sharing of lessons learned.

## Foster Psychological Safety in Meetings

Leaders should recognize the immense impact of meetings on team dynamics and create meeting spaces where everyone's voice is heard, and ideas are welcomed without judgment. Leaders must actively listen to diverse perspectives, validate contributions, and ensure that all team members feel valued and respected during discussions.

## Provide Training and Support

You can't get there without change. Building psychological safety requires intentional effort. Leaders invest in training – refer to the appendix for specific components to include in your training program. Support and equip team members with the skills to navigate feedback conversations effectively. Workshops, coaching sessions, and resources on providing and receiving feedback are available to empower individuals to engage in constructive and growth-oriented feedback exchanges. Make it part of the culture – lead.

## Listening with Empathy: The Resonance of Genuine Connection

Within the symphony of psychological safety, the art of empathetic listening emerges as a harmonious melody that weaves together the fabric of trust and understanding. Like skilled conductors, leaders and team members master this art, conducting conversations with the baton of empathy and orchestrating profound connections.

### The Power of Being Heard and Understood

In the realm of psychological safety, every voice finds a receptive ear. Listening with empathy becomes critical, where individuals feel truly seen and understood. As team members share their thoughts, ideas, and concerns, empathetic listeners immerse themselves in the symphony of emotions, acknowledging the depth of each sentiment.

Empathy sets the stage for an enchanting dance of active participation in feedback conversations. When individuals feel that their contributions matter, they become willing dancers, gracefully engaging in the choreography of dialogue. Empathetic listeners do not merely hear the words; they tune into the nuances, the emotions that thread through the conversations, and the unspoken hopes and fears that linger in the background.

Empathy weaves with golden threads of understanding and compassion. Leaders and team members embrace trust, fostering a sense of belonging and camaraderie within the team. This sense of belonging propels individuals to give their best, knowing their efforts and aspirations are appreciated.

The emphasis on being heard and understood aligns with psychological theories on the importance of validation and empathy in human interactions. For instance, Maslow's Hierarchy of Needs emphasizes the need for belonging and love. When individuals feel genuinely heard and understood, they fulfill these social needs, enhancing their overall well-being and motivation. Empathy, a key component of emotional intelligence, allows individuals to connect on a deeper level, strengthening relationships and building trust. Empathetic listening encourages reciprocity, leading to more open and meaningful conversations.

## Learning from Mistakes: Cultivating a Growth-Oriented Mindset

Within the sanctuary of psychological safety, a profound transformation occurs - the metamorphosis of mistakes from burdens of shame to growth opportunities. Individuals no longer fear missteps but embrace them as necessary components of their journey. They understand that perfection is a mirage and the path to greatness is paved with imperfect steps of progress.

In the embrace of psychological safety, the art of acknowledgment unfolds. Individuals feel liberated to stand in the light of truth, admitting their misjudgments, miscalculations, and missed opportunities. They look for lessons learned and identify their own weaknesses and blind spots.

## Feedback as the Mirror of Reflection

Here is where feedback takes on a new role - that of a reflective mirror that reveals the lessons hidden within mistakes. Individuals eagerly seek feedback not to validate their accomplishments but to discover the untapped potential within their missteps. They uncover insights and perspectives that would have remained obscured without psychological safety.

Givers of feedback become beacons of encouragement, illuminating the path of growth for the receivers. Their words, laced with compassion, guide individuals toward introspection and self-improvement. Feedback, once seen as a source of trepidation, now becomes a source of inspiration, a guidepost towards transformation.

In the garden of psychological safety, resilience sprouts and flourishes. Individuals understand that setbacks are not final verdicts but a learning detour toward success. They learn to dust themselves off, rise from the fall, and embrace the wisdom gained from each experience.

## The Journey of Growth

As we traverse the landscape of psychological safety, a growth-oriented mindset takes root, bearing the fruits of courage, resilience, and continuous improvement. We celebrate the transformation of errors into opportunities, where the language of feedback nurtures growth and empowers individuals to embrace their journey with open hearts and minds.

## A Feedback Culture of Empowerment: Nurturing Growth Together

In the heart of every thriving organization lies a powerful force - a feedback culture that breathes life into everyone's potential and elevates the collective spirit. A feedback culture transcends the mere exchange of words, it becomes a catalyst for empowerment and growth.

In this culture of empowerment, courage, and vulnerability dance hand in hand. Individuals no longer shy away from feedback; they embrace it as a gift of growth. The fear of judgment dissolves as the nurturing embrace of psychological safety envelops them. Every interaction becomes an opportunity for growth. Feedback is no longer confined to formal performance reviews; it permeates the fabric of daily interactions. From casual hallway conversations to team meetings, feedback becomes a natural aspect of communication, fostering a continuous improvement mindset.

Empowerment spreads like ripples on a calm lake, touching every corner of the organization. As individuals are emboldened to take ownership of their growth, they inspire others to do the same. Feedback becomes a collective journey, where each person's progress uplifts the entire team and organization.

## Leaders as Champions of Empowerment

Leaders, by example, must embrace feedback with humility and gratitude. In doing so, they foster an environment where team members feel safe to express their thoughts, ideas, and concerns. Leaders understand that their role extends beyond offering feedback; they are enablers of growth, igniting the spark of potential in every individual.

With psychological safety as its core, transformative change flourishes. The organization becomes a dynamic ecosystem, constantly adapting and evolving. Feedback guides individuals and teams toward their shared vision and purpose. Growth is no longer a distant destination but a continuous exploration and progress journey.

# CHAPTER 6: FEEDBACK TOOLS AND TECHNOLOGIES - THE DOUBLE-EDGED SWORD

## Introduction

In an increasingly digital world, Feedback Tools and Technologies have revolutionized how organizations manage performance, development, and communication. They offer a seemingly unending repository of insights, allowing managers and employees to tap into valuable perspectives at scale. But this convenience comes at a price. As these tools grow more prevalent, we must ask: Are we sacrificing the nuance and human connection that face-to-face feedback provides?

## The Allure of Anonymity

One of the significant features that many Feedback Tools offer is anonymity. This can be incredibly liberating for employees who might not feel comfortable giving honest feedback in a face-to-face setting. Anonymity removes the fear of potential repercussions, allowing more open and honest opinions.

While anonymity can encourage candor, it can also foster a lack of accountability. Anonymous feedback can sometimes become a breeding ground for destructive comments, stripped of constructive intent. The human element, characterized by empathy and understanding, can often be lost, leaving recipients with feedback that feels cold, impersonal, or harmful.

## The Efficiency Paradox

Feedback Tools and Technologies are unparalleled when it comes to efficiency. They can aggregate data, identify trends, and offer 'smart' suggestions based on pre-determined criteria. Manual methods of feedback collection can hardly match this sort of efficiency.

But what happens when feedback becomes a box-ticking exercise? When it's just a matter of clicking predefined options or sliding a scale from 1 to 10? The convenience of these tools can dilute the quality of feedback. The warmth of a vocal tone, the encouragement of a smile, or the compassion in someone's eyes are irreplaceable facets of human communication that technology can't replicate. They offer context and texture that a written comment or a numeric score simply can't capture.

## A Symphony of Voices

Feedback tools offer us the advantage of gathering many perspectives almost effortlessly. 360-degree feedback, peer reviews, and self-assessments can all be seamlessly integrated, providing a well-rounded view of performance.

However, the influx of data points can sometimes turn feedback into a statistical exercise devoid of personal touch. When feedback becomes a pie chart or a performance graph, the individual nuances can get overshadowed. No graph can capture the intangible qualities that make each employee unique, nor can it encapsulate the complexities of human emotion and aspiration often underpinning performance metrics.

## Striking a Balance

It would be impractical, even foolish, to disregard the many advantages Feedback Tools and Technologies brings. However, as we integrate these tools into our feedback culture, it's crucial to remain mindful of what we might be giving up in exchange for efficiency and scale. The challenge, then, is to strike a balance: to use these tools as a supplement to human interaction, not a replacement.

By combining the irreplaceable aspects of human communication with the scale and efficiency that technology offers, we can cultivate a feedback culture rich in quality and reach. In this dance between technology and human connection, we must find a rhythm that embraces the strengths of both.

## Embracing the Digital Feedback Ecosystem

As organizations continue their digital transformation, feedback mechanisms have found a new dimension. Online surveys, feedback portals, and mobile applications have become invaluable tools in gathering feedback from employees, customers, and stakeholders. These digital avenues streamline the feedback collection process, providing real-time insights that inform decision-making at every level.

Technology empowers feedback givers and receivers with data-driven insights. Advanced analytics and sentiment analysis techniques process vast amounts of feedback data, unveiling patterns, trends, and sentiments that might have otherwise remained hidden. These data-driven insights paint a comprehensive picture of the organization's strengths, areas for improvement, and emerging opportunities, serving as a compass for strategic growth.

However, its value can only be realized when coupled with thoughtful and personalized delivery. Digital platforms allow feedback givers to provide specific, actionable insights backed by data and evidence. The human touch is not lost but rather augmented, as technology enables feedback givers to focus on the areas that matter most, amplifying the impact of their guidance.

As remote work and global collaboration become commonplace, technology bridges geographical divides, fostering a global feedback culture. Virtual meetings, video conferencing, and collaboration tools empower teams to share feedback effortlessly across borders and time zones. The exchange of ideas becomes borderless, enhancing cultural understanding and celebrating diverse perspectives.

## The Role of Artificial Intelligence (AI)

AI is emerging as a game-changer in the feedback landscape. AI-powered chatbots and virtual assistants facilitate real-time feedback interactions, enhancing accessibility and responsiveness. Additionally, AI-driven language processing tools aid in crafting constructive and empathetic feedback, ensuring that the right message is conveyed with clarity and sensitivity.

Remember, while technology accelerates feedback processes, balancing efficiency and human connection is essential. Feedback must remain a meaningful and authentic exchange, not merely a checkbox on a digital form. Organizations must infuse the feedback process with empathy and understanding, remembering that behind each data point lies a unique individual seeking growth and support.

As we explore the potential of feedback technologies, ethical considerations emerge. Organizations must prioritize data privacy and security, ensuring that feedback data is handled responsibly and transparently. The ethical use of AI and data analytics should prioritize individual well-being and never compromise human dignity.

# CHAPTER 7: FEEDBACK AND ORGANIZATIONAL PERFORMANCE

Welcome to the world of vibrant workplaces, where employees are more than just cogs in a machine. Picture an office buzzing with energy, where people aren't just punching the clock but are deeply involved in purposeful work. In such an atmosphere, feedback isn't a dreaded event but an ongoing dialogue. Sit back, sip on your favorite brew, and delve into how a rich feedback culture can make this dream a reality for your organization.

## Unlocking Productivity through Feedback

In workplaces prioritizing feedback, employees are not working in a vacuum but in tune with organizational goals. The clarity and purpose from regular, actionable feedback enable them to continually hone their skills and align their work with the broader vision, thereby driving productivity.

## Making Performance Management Effective

Gone are the days when performance reviews were annual, anxiety-inducing events. In a feedback-centric culture, assessments are ongoing conversations, facilitating immediate improvements and targeted skill development.

## Fostering Engagement and Job Satisfaction

Nothing screams 'you belong here' louder than an environment where each voice is heard and valued. When feedback is the norm, employees feel a stronger sense of connection to the organizational mission and their team members. This enhances job satisfaction and fosters a climate of mutual respect and collaboration.

### Retention and Skill Development: Two Sides of the Same Coin

Keeping employees engaged is crucial in a world where skilled employees have no dearth of opportunities. A workplace that actively encourages feedback sends a clear message: "Your growth is our growth." Such an approach not only aids retention but provides a tailored roadmap for employee development.

### Building a Feedback-Driven Culture

Commitment to fostering a feedback-driven culture is paramount. Leaders must set an example by actively seeking and receiving feedback and demonstrating a growth mindset. Regular training sessions can also arm your workforce with the skills to effectively give and receive feedback. Let's examine a few case studies into the positive results of constructive feedback.

Example 1: Company ABC faced significant challenges: declining performance, disengaged employees, and a lack of innovation. Recognizing the urgent need for change, the company leadership implemented a comprehensive feedback system fostering open communication and empowering employees to share their ideas and concerns.

Implementing the feedback system was more than just a top-down initiative. It involved creating a culture where every individual's voice was valued and heard. By encouraging open communication at all levels of the organization, leaders provided a safe space for employees to express their thoughts and opinions freely. This open communication nurtured a sense of psychological safety, where employees felt comfortable sharing their successes and challenges.

With the newfound platform for open communication, the company tapped into a wellspring of untapped potential – its workforce's creativity and innovative ideas. Employees felt empowered to propose new solutions, suggest process improvements, and contribute ideas previously left unheard. This unleashed a wave of innovation throughout the organization, driving the development of new products, services, and strategies that provided a competitive edge.

Leaders witnessed efficiency and overall performance improvements as the feedback system matured. The continuous feedback loop allowed individuals to identify and address inefficiencies promptly. Feedback provided a real-time mechanism for course correction, leading to streamlined processes, reduced waste, and improved productivity. Employees felt a sense of ownership over their work and performance, knowing their feedback contributed to the company's success.

The culture cultivated a growth mindset among employees. Feedback was no longer perceived as criticism but as an opportunity for learning and development. Instead of feeling discouraged by feedback, employees embraced it with a growth-oriented attitude, eager to learn from their experiences and improve continuously.

As the feedback culture took root and flourished, the company experienced a transformational turnaround. The organization's once-struggling performance now soared to new heights. The combination of open communication, unleashed innovation, enhanced efficiency, and a growth mindset propelled the organization toward success. Employee engagement and satisfaction levels rose significantly, reducing turnover and increasing loyalty.

This transformational turnaround is a powerful testament to the impact of a robust feedback culture. By prioritizing open communication and empowerment, the organization harnessed the collective potential of its workforce, leading to innovation, efficiency, and remarkable performance improvements.

Example 2: Company XYZ committed to emphasizing employee development through regular feedback and coaching sessions. They recognized the critical role of employee development in driving organizational success. To achieve this, the company implemented a formal feedback and coaching system that strongly emphasized aligning feedback with employees' career aspirations.

Feedback was not a mere performance evaluation tool but a means to empower employees' growth and development. Regular feedback and coaching sessions were conducted to provide employees with valuable insights into their strengths and areas for improvement. The personalized feedback sessions focused on each employee's career goals and aspirations.

The feedback was tailored to each employee's unique career journey. Managers took the time to understand their team members' long-term goals and provided feedback that would contribute to their professional growth. This personalized approach made employees feel seen, valued, and supported, motivating them to excel in their roles and beyond.

The emphasis on employee development created a culture of learning and growth. Employees were encouraged to embrace feedback as an opportunity for skill enhancement and personal improvement. Rather than feeling apprehensive about feedback, employees welcomed it as a chance to improve and progress in their careers continuously.

The feedback and coaching system significantly impacted employee engagement and retention. Employees felt a sense of investment from the company in their professional development, which boosted their commitment and loyalty. The culture of learning and growth resulted in a more motivated and satisfied workforce, leading to reduced turnover rates and increased productivity.

As word spread about the company's commitment to employee development and growth-oriented feedback, it became an employer of choice. Talented individuals sought opportunities to join the organization, attracted by the prospect of working in an environment that genuinely valued and nurtured its employees.

The focus on empowering employee growth through feedback and coaching sessions demonstrated the transformative impact of personalized and career-aligned feedback. By fostering a culture of learning and development, the company improved employee engagement and retention and positioned itself as a sought-after employer in the industry. This is an inspiring example of how organizations can leverage feedback to empower their employees and drive organizational excellence.

Measuring to Improve

What gets measured gets managed. For organizations committed to establishing a feedback-rich culture, metrics like employee satisfaction surveys, performance evaluations, and turnover rates serve as invaluable indicators. These measurements aren't just numbers; they offer insights for refining your feedback mechanisms and identifying the areas that need attention.

Employee satisfaction surveys - are essential to gauge how employees perceive the feedback they receive and the overall effectiveness of the feedback process. These surveys can be conducted periodically, providing a pulse on the organization's feedback culture and identifying areas for improvement.

Performance evaluations - also serve as a critical feedback metric, offering a comprehensive view of how feedback has influenced individual and team performance. By analyzing performance data over time, organizations can identify trends and patterns that indicate the effectiveness of their feedback practices.

Employee turnover rates - are another significant feedback metric. High turnover rates suggest issues with the feedback culture, where employees might feel undervalued or unsupported. On the other hand, low turnover rates can indicate a thriving feedback culture that nurtures talent and encourages long-term commitment.

Continuous Improvement: The data gathered from feedback metrics is pivotal in driving ongoing improvement efforts. Organizations can use feedback data to identify strengths and weaknesses in their feedback processes and make strategic decisions accordingly. For instance, if employee satisfaction survey results highlight dissatisfaction with the feedback process, leaders can implement targeted training sessions for feedback providers or explore new tools and technologies.

By analyzing performance evaluation data, organizations can identify areas where employees excel and areas that require improvement. These insights can inform training and development initiatives, enabling employees to focus on enhancing their skills and competencies.

Feedback data can also be used to spot trends in employee turnover. If specific teams or departments experience higher turnover rates, leaders can investigate the underlying causes and take corrective actions. Addressing these issues can contribute to increased employee satisfaction and retention. In this section, we unveil the transformative potential of a feedback-rich culture on organizational performance, employee engagement, and talent retention. Through real-life examples of successful feedback implementations, we showcase how organizations can leverage feedback to elevate their performance.

## The Transformative Potential of Feedback

Whether it's becoming more agile or more attuned to employee needs, the benefits are transformative and far-reaching. The era of keeping feedback in the shadows is over. Companies that are willing to make feedback an integral part of their culture are reaping manifold benefits, from higher productivity and engagement to greater retention of talent. It's high time to join the feedback revolution and unlock the collective potential of your organization.

# CHAPTER 8: EMBRACING THE EVOLUTION OF FEEDBACK

As we reach the conclusion of this transformative journey, we are reminded of the profound impact feedback can have on individuals and organizations alike. Throughout this book, " Feedback is Not a Gift, it is a Minefield," we have explored the intricacies of feedback and unraveled the layers that make it a powerful tool. It is time to approach feedback with a sense of caution, aware of its powerful nature for growth and destruction.

In our exploration, we have recognized that feedback is not a one-size-fits-all concept. It is a multifaceted and nuanced process that requires careful consideration and skillful execution. The traditional notion of feedback as a gift has little merit and falls short when we fail to address its complexities. We have learned that feedback can be a double-edged sword, capable of uplifting or wounding depending on its delivery and intent.

Our journey has taken us through the various layers of effective feedback, from the importance of specificity and clarity to the role of psychological safety in empowering both givers and receivers. We have witnessed the transformational power of constructive criticism and the significance of embracing vulnerability and trust in feedback exchanges.

Furthermore, we have explored the role of technology in enhancing feedback mechanisms, acknowledging that online surveys, feedback portals, and mobile applications can provide invaluable real-time insights to inform decision-making at every level.

Through examples and case studies, we have witnessed the impact of a healthy feedback culture on organizational performance, employee engagement, and talent retention. We have seen how organizations that prioritize feedback and value continuous improvement are more likely to thrive in an ever-changing business landscape.

Armed with the tools and insights this book shares, it is time for managers, leaders, and employees to take charge of feedback and shape it into a force for positive change. We must challenge the status quo and move beyond the illusion of surface-level feedback. Instead, let us embrace feedback as a vehicle for authentic growth and development.

To foster a culture of continuous learning and success, we must listen with empathy, adapt feedback to different learning styles, and recognize the significance of constructive criticism in guiding individuals toward their full potential.

As we conclude this journey, we are reminded that feedback is not a static concept; it evolves with us and our organizations. By embracing this evolution and valuing feedback as a catalyst for transformation, we create an environment where individuals and teams flourish, and success becomes a collective journey.

In the ever-evolving landscape of business and personal growth, let us continue to learn, adapt, and embrace the power of feedback. By doing so, we pave the way for a future where feedback is not just a gift but a cherished tool that empowers us to reach new heights of excellence. Together, let us embark on this exciting journey of growth and possibility fueled by the evolution of feedback.

# APPENDIX

**FEEDBACK TRAINING**

When considering training courses to create or improve your feedback culture, remember that creating a psychologically safe environment for feedback requires a comprehensive approach considering the multiple facets of organizational culture, interpersonal dynamics, and individual behavior. The following is breakdown of the training components needed to foster such an environment:

### Understanding Psychological Safety:

Definition, significance, and benefits.

Recognizing the symptoms of a psychologically unsafe environment.

Real-life examples and case studies.

### Effective Communication Skills:

Active listening techniques.

Constructive feedback delivery.

Asking open-ended questions to encourage dialogue.

Avoiding blame language and focusing on behavior over personality.

### Empathy and Emotional Intelligence:

Recognizing and validating others' feelings.

Managing and regulating one's own emotions.

Understanding non-verbal cues and body language.

### Conflict Resolution Techniques:

Identifying sources of conflict.

Mediation and negotiation skills.

Creating win-win situations.

**Building Trust:**

Consistency in actions and follow-through.

Honesty and transparency in interactions.

Understanding and respecting boundaries.

**Inclusivity and Diversity Training:**

Recognizing unconscious biases.

Valuing different perspectives and experiences.

Building a culture of respect irrespective of background or position.

**Leadership Training:**

Leading by example to foster psychological safety.

Being approachable and encouraging open dialogue.

Celebrating vulnerability as a strength.

**Feedback Frameworks and Models:**

Best practices for giving and receiving feedback.

Understanding the impact of positive reinforcement.

Using feedback models like "Situation, Behavior, Impact" or "Start, Stop, Continue."

**Encouraging Reporting:**

Making it safe for employees to report issues or concerns.

Ensuring confidentiality and non-retaliation for reporting.

Having clear protocols for addressing reports.

**Regular Check-ins and Surveys:**

Tools and techniques for gauging psychological safety in teams.

Analyzing and acting upon survey feedback.

**Case Studies and Role-playing:**

Practical exercises to simulate real-life situations.

Analyzing scenarios and discussing optimal responses.

**Ongoing Support and Resources:**

Establishing mentorship or coaching programs.

Offering resources like counseling for employees facing challenges.

Continuous training and refresher courses.

It's crucial to note that training alone isn't enough to ensure psychological safety. An organization's leadership must be genuinely committed to these principles, ensuring they're embedded in the company's culture and values. Regular evaluations and adaptations are also vital to maintain and improve the state of psychological safety over time.

## MEMORY TOOLS

Memory tricks can be incredibly useful for ingraining important principles. Below are a few acronyms to help remember the key aspects of creating a psychologically safe feedback culture:

## S.A.F.E.T.Y.

- **S**: **Seek** understanding. Before giving feedback, ensure you understand the situation fully. When receiving, aim to comprehend the giver's perspective.

- **A**: **Ask** open-ended questions. This encourages a dialogue where both parties can share their perspectives.

- **F**: **Focus** on behavior, not the person. Feedback should be about specific actions or outcomes, not personal attributes.

- **E: Empathize**. Put yourself in the other person's shoes. Recognize and validate feelings, even if you don't agree with them.

- **T: Thank** the other person. Whether you're giving or receiving feedback, showing appreciation fosters mutual respect.

- **Y: Yield** a two-way conversation. Feedback isn't just a monologue; allow space for the receiver to share thoughts, feelings, and perspectives.

By keeping S.A.F.E.T.Y. in mind, individuals can remember the critical aspects of fostering a psychologically safe environment for feedback.

## F.E.E.D.B.A.C.K.

- **F: Fairness**. Ensure your feedback is impartial, unbiased, and fair to all involved.

- **E: Empowerment**. Construct your feedback to enable and empower the recipient to take positive action.

- **E: Evidence-Based**. Ground your feedback in clear examples or evidence to prevent it from feeling like a personal attack.

- **D: Dialogue**. Encourage two-way communication and be open to hearing the recipient's perspective.

- **B: Balanced**. Combine both positive remarks with areas of improvement to provide a holistic view.

- **A: Action-Oriented**. Make your feedback actionable. Offer solutions or suggestions where possible.

- **C: Compassionate**. Deliver feedback with kindness,

understanding the recipient's feelings and perspective.

- **K: Knowledgeable**. Ensure you are informed about the situation, context, and subject matter before offering feedback.

By recalling F.E.E.D.B.A.C.K., individuals can maintain a structured and positive approach when navigating feedback conversations in a psychologically safe environment.

### Feedback Rhyme

Feedback, feedback on the wall,

Who's the fairest of them all?

Not the one who speaks with spite,

But the one who gets feedback right.

Listen close, speak with care,

Make sure your intentions are clear and fair.

For feedback's gift is not to blame,

But to help us all up our game.

So next time you speak, take a beat,

Ensure your feedback's constructive and sweet.

For in the world of give and take,

Feedback's how we grow and create!

*Ok, perhaps I'm more of a writer than a poet - now I know.*

Thank you for joining me on this exploration of feedback's transformative potential. Remember, with the power of feedback comes the responsibility to wield it wisely. Let us all be both courageous in giving, and gracious in receiving, as we navigate the intricate dance of human connection. Let us move forward together.

*Where there is great power, there is great responsibility* - Winston Churchill, who said it before Uncle Ben on Spiderman.

# ACKNOWLEDGEMENT

First and foremost, I owe gratitude to the men and women I served alongside in the United States Navy. The discipline, resilience, and camaraderie I learned at sea have been my steadfast compass throughout life's journey.

To my mentors in technology and business—your wisdom and guidance have been invaluable. You've shown me that knowledge is power and a gift to be shared. Special thanks to my colleagues at the corporations and Higher-Ed institutions I've worked for; your challenges and support have made me a better professional and human being. Well, some of them have - some induced therapy but I got over it. Or did I?

A heartfelt thank you to my entrepreneurial peers and family who have been part of the journey. You've taught me that the spirit of entrepreneurship is a group event and your faith and support in my ideas have sometimes surpassed my own. See Deb, I told you it would be fun.

A special shoutout to my southern family and friends for instilling a love of barbeque, sweet tea, humor, and a knack for storytelling.

And to you, dear reader—thank you for walking this path with me. Whether you've picked up this book seeking knowledge, inspiration, or just a good read, I hope you find what you're looking for and much more.

Here's to pursuing your passion.  Eat, drink, and enjoy life.

With heartfelt thanks,

JD Ussery

# ABOUT THE AUTHOR

## Jd Ussery

JD Ussery is not your average Southern gentleman—though his love for sweet tea and humor remains steadfast. This multi-hyphenate personality has carved a life as varied as it is fulfilling, with each chapter building on the lessons of the last. A Navy veteran who has sailed the oceans, JD has a unique blend of discipline and adventurous spirit that took him from the expansive waters of the world to the intricate landscapes of advanced electronics.

He honed his computer expertise at IBM, skillfully navigating network and systems engineering realms. His managerial roles are a testament to a leadership style deeply rooted in collaboration and empowerment, principles he further honed as an Associate Chief Information Officer at a large SEC university.

But JD's technical and leadership acumen is only part of his story. An avid entrepreneur, he's turned his flair for innovation into various successful businesses. Not content to keep his insights to himself, JD offers humor, wisdom, and experience to help uplift peers, teammates, and anyone seeking his counsel.

As a technical writer turned author, JD finds his truest expression in the written word. He doesn't just write; he explores the boundless territories of passion and purpose, urging his readers to do the same. Whether he's penning a technical manual or an inspirational tome, or consulting on an entrepreneurial opportunity, JD Ussery is a master at weaving life's complexities into narratives that not only inform but inspire. In both life and literature, he embodies a timeless lesson: pursuing passion is the greatest voyage of all.

# KEEP THE CONVERSATION GOING

Did this book strike a chord with you? If so, I'd be honored if you'd share it with a friend or two.

I'd love to hear your thoughts as well. A review on Amazon not only helps me, but it also helps potential readers decide whether this book is the right fit for them. Your voice matters, so make it heard!

**Let's Stay Connected**: For the latest updates, exclusive content, and a deeper dive into my creative world, bookmark my author website: jdussery.com.

**Let's Chat:** Questions? Comments? Just want to talk about the book? I'm an email away, and I'd love to hear from you: jd@jdussery.com.

Thank you for your support! Let us both continue onward and upward!

JD

# PROSE & PONDERINGS

## My Other Works

**Espresso Express** - Your Ultimate Guide to Launching a Successful Mobile Coffee Shop

**Ice Cold Entrepreneurship** - Launching Your Shaved Ice Business

**Ca$h In On ChatGPT: From Novice To Mogul** - How to Monetize with ChatGPT

**Feedback is Not a Gift, It is a Minefield** - How to create a positive environment for constructive feedback.

**From My Blog -** https://jdussery.com/blog/

Printed in Great Britain
by Amazon

33120915R00056